You Found Me

A collection of poems

Manjishtha Pahilajani

BookLeaf Publishing

India | USA | UK

Made with ❤ on the BookLeaf Publishing Platform
www.bookleafpub.in
www.bookleafpub.com

Dedication

To you, dear reader,

This book holds pieces of me – moments I couldn't keep to myself, questions I'm still figuring out, half-learned lessons and a few stories I thought were worth sharing. Each poem is an offering, a glimpse into my world and perhaps a mirror to your own. I hope to meet you somewhere between the pages and your interpretation.

With love and vulnerability,

Manjishtha

Acknowledgements

First and foremost, I am immensely grateful to BookLeaf Publishing for creating this 21-day challenge, inspiring me and helping me bring this creation to life.

To everyone who has ever inspired a poem, knowingly or unknowingly, this collection exists because of you.

To my family, for their love and lessons, all of which are woven into my words. You've given me stories to tell and a safe place to return to.

To my friends, for being my chosen family, and for the laughs, heartbreaks and memories that shaped so many verses.

To the readers, for taking the time to sit with my words. Your presence here is a gift I will never take lightly.

To the ones who stayed, the ones who left, and the ones I'm yet to meet – thank you for being part of the mosaic of my life.

And finally, to the version of me who decided to pick up the pen and write: you were brave, and I'm proud of you.

Preface

This collection is my way of crawling out of a very long writer's block– unsure of how it will turn out but determined to try.

What I hope to achieve here is twofold: to reconnect with my creative and curious side as well as to share pieces of myself I've discovered (and rediscovered) during my 20-something years on this earth in the hopes that someone, somewhere, felt the same at some point in their lives

These poems are as much for you as they are for me. I hope this book acts as a mirror – sometimes clear, other times cracked or distorted – but always reflecting something, whether about me, you or both. And if nothing else, I hope it's a piece of art that makes you pause, think, or feel, even for a moment.

Thank you for letting these words into your world.

See you on the other side of the mirror,
Manjishtha

11/11. Make a Wish

I used to make bigger wishes when I was small
like world peace or ending poverty.
but as I grew older, my wishes got smaller
and little more realistic, more selfish perhaps?
maybe it's because god became more human
in my eyes and my eyelashes fell faster
and I couldn't lose more 11:11s to wishes
trying to cure man-made issues.
so I sometimes asked for happiness
for someone who was close to me
and who was struggling at the time
and sometimes that was me
'Please just this one thing,
it's urgent, and you know this feeling.
I know I've asked for many things over the years
and you have to deal with humanity's biggest fears
but right now they (I) need it
and they (I) could use a breather from destiny
I won't promise this is my last wish
but it's making my heart itch
Which is not bigger than world peace or poverty
but might save one person's sanity'.

12/11. Care Label

tearing at the inseams of my soul
looking for a label that will tell me
how to take care of it
should I wash it in the machine or with hands?
iron the wrinkles or dry clean?
is bleaching the stains an option?
maybe I should look for its origin.
was it made by over-exploited workers
which is why it's worn out at 22?
or was it a high-quality brand
that the owner didn't take care of properly?
I think the only instruction that comes with it is
'handle with care'

13/11. The Orange Peel Theory

an interesting and trendy concept on Instagram
is a lived reality for many who refuse to see it.
my mother peels, not only oranges
but also pomegranates for me,
every day without fail.
I know it's not the love you all talk about
but that's not the orange peel theory.
it's pure, unadulterated love you receive
from anyone in any form
and gratitude comes hard to those fooled by society
into believing that fairytales require a partner
but does it not matter that
your mother doesn't want you to go to work hungry?
your friend thinks of you in middle of boring classes?
your grandfather is putting all his energy into that
tiny tangerine for you?
your sibling gives you a slice after a fight?
the orange peel theory rests solely on the fact
that someone, somewhere,
would take out a little time,
make a little effort, put a little thought
and perform this small but intimate form of service
for you

14/11. Children's Day

children don't need a day
it's us adults who need a children's day–
to be able to have the same curiosity,
the same desire for life's offerings,
the same simplicity of love,
the same priorities of wanting
to be seen, heard, loved and understood
and nothing beyond.
the same understanding of the universe
that each day is our gift to be cherished
and every little act of kindness
needs appreciation,
acknowledgement,
and reciprocation.
the same self-awareness
'I'm good at drawing
but I'm still learning to cycle'
we need to go back to that,
even if for a day.
I think trying to make the world
more complicated as we grow
makes life more difficult.
the simple truth that–
life is to be lived
is known to us in childhood
and fades in our minds as we grow.
so, every children's day
meet your inner child
you'd find the joie de vivre you left behind.

15/11. In Sickness And In Health

if you can promise that
to your loved ones
why not to yourself?
your body has carried
you through the years of life.
your mind has in it
a myriad of experiences, emotions
people, places and lessons
saved in its depths
and it hasn't crashed.
I think if they ask for a little breather–
so let the self-critic save its breath,
even for a moment.
you don't scream at a loved one
when they're having a breakdown,
so consider yourself a loved one
And promise yourself this–
'in sickness and in health,
until death do us part.
I will love and honour you
all the days of my life'.

16/11. A Degree In Being Human

I think you learn a thing or two
when you're two degrees into life
I mean, not to brag but I know a lot about people
now,
living in unknown cities; scratch that, countries
actually!
and the human mind and behaviour
is vast and complex and grey.
I know for sure,
there are no heroes or villains in real life,
only humans who make choices
that makes them a hero or a villain
at that juncture of their lives
in those people's eyes.
and then you grow and change and evolve
if you choose to learn from those experiences
for better or for worse.
to be human is to dream, love and hope.
to be human is to make mistakes, hurt and get hurt.
to be human is to succeed, fail and try.
to be human is to have a family to lean on.
to be human is to have enemies and lovers
and lovers to enemies and enemies to lovers
and strangers to friends and friends to family
but also friends to strangers.

regardless, life goes on,
what you plan may not happen
who you plan your life with may not stay
where you plan to be isn't where you might end up
And it feels great to hope
that things will go according to plan one day
but isn't it so much better to just live
and be human?

17/11. The Geography Of Me

This lesson starts two generations before me.

I have inherited the culture of a place
neither I nor my parents have ever been to.
You see, we carry Sindhi blood in our veins
and reside in post-partition India.
So now, the birthplace of my culture
is in a so-called 'enemy' country.

But the beauty of a displaced community
is that we value culture so much more,
carrying it with pride as the last remnant
of a beautiful, uncolonised, vibrant identity.

The next chapter begins with my mother,
who came from the Pink City
to the Capital City to meet my dad,
and then we finally settled
in the Millennium City of India.

Skip forward to my master's degree–
starting from the Lion City,
ending in the City of Gold,
and then back to my Hometown.

And even though I hated Geography as a subject,
my own life has been a masterclass in it,
crossing borders and barriers,
spanning so many cities and countries,

that pieces of everywhere are in me,
and pieces of me are everywhere I've been
and in the culture, I carry from places I've never seen

18/11. Things Tell Tales

Minimalism sounds great; in theory,
but it's not for me.
I have a crab keychain
with a tiny attached comb
that no longer fits in my hair,
but it's from my grandmother,
so I've kept it safe for childhood's sake.
I have handmade birthday cards
from school friends I've lost touch with.
I have diary entries from family
that became strangers.
I have polaroids of friends
who I fought with and pushed away.
I have broken necklaces
that were gifts to me.
I have terrible arts and crafts projects
that cost sleepless nights.
I have keychains that I don't have keys for.
I collect stamps,
but I've never written a letter.
I have vinyl records,
but the player doesn't work anymore.
I have board games with missing pieces,
I have stray cards that found their way out of a set.

I have so many things with no practical use
other than telling me stories of my life—
a time capsule of a memory I wanted to cherish,
whether joyful, bittersweet or devastating.

I think that's the curse of a writer:
you can never stop looking for stories.
And things tell tales.

19/11. Rest In Peace

I have never been good at running–
physically. But in life?
I've always been running:
towards something,
away from something,
or just running like a hamster in a wheel,
because I feel like I'm supposed to.

Hustle culture is so deeply ingrained
that anything other than constant motion,
constant grind, feels unfathomable.
In a world like this, rest is evil.
Rest is lazy,
it's wasteful, tasteless.
there's only rest when it's over–
rest that is eternal.
but let's be real:
when you're running,
you don't see your surroundings.
you don't focus on how you feel,
or listen to what your body is trying to tell you.
you don't have time for the people next to you.
if they're running, they're competition.
if they're not, they're forgotten.

So what's the big prize?
the thing you're making all these sacrifices for?
why are you dashing through life
towards things you think
will make it better,
but not stopping to actually live it?

'I'll rest when I'm dead'.
but you'll die when you're dead.
Rest is for the living.
I know there's a million things you haven't done yet,
but resting for a moment won't stop your progress.
It'll help you see how far you've come—
and give you the courage to keep going.

20/11. I Think I Love You

This is not a love story
till you consent, dear reader.
but I feel the way I talk to you
is the most vulnerable I've ever been.

So here I am, taking a midway break
to say: I think I love you.
and I think you found me–
wandering in these pages.

If you've made it this far,
maybe you love me too,
or at least, my poems.

and isn't that the same for every poet, every writer?
To love the art is to love the artist.

So, do you?

21/11. Friendship Breakup

High time someone
wrote a poem about
the worst kind of breakups–
the platonic ones,
the ones with the ones
who were supposed to be there forever,
to be by your side just to talk, laugh and cry.

How is it that someone who knew your soul
would now hesitate to say hi if you met?
And isn't it even worse knowing
it wasn't one person, but both of you
who failed the simplest task–
being there for each other?

Shouldn't the greatest of poets
talk about friends who turned into family,
then to strangers in just one lifetime?
You chose each other over and over again,
and they knew what kind of soulmate you'd marry,
and you knew who was their knight in shining
armour.

But none of that matters now,
because, for the last time,
you didn't choose each other.

Isn't that as tragic, if not more,
than a romantic breakup?
You could date someone new
after breaking up with your partner,
but can you still make a new best friend
who will care enough to do a PhD
on your childhood, likes, dislikes,
secrets, desires, dreams,
fears, passions and love,
and dutifully pass on the information
to your romantic partners?

I don't know how to get over this.
I can't stop thinking about them
when their favourite song plays,
or when I see a meme they'd laugh at,
or when I meet a person they'd hate.
I can't stop imagining the day
we cross paths again
and have to pretend
you never promised each other
to stick around forever.

22/11. People Leaf

I think fall is a seasonal lesson
in letting go.
Leaves falling,
like people leaving.

The tree is hurt,
and the branches tired.
You want to hold on,
but you can't.

They're meant for the wind,
and you must let go–
make space
for new foliage,
new people,
new seasons of life.

23/11. For Dadu

I never expected things
to come to a close like this–
there, and then gone.

I was grieving in a different country,
mourning a person who cared for me and my siblings,
through childhood and well into adulthood.
Just gone one day–
and a phone call to verify it.

I heard that even in his last days,
he told everyone he was proud of me.
But the guilt does not leave.
Nor does the grief.

That was the day I started
believing in God and afterlife again.
Because when I went to a temple and prayed,
something heavy lifted off of me–
as if I was letting go of his soul
in a place he was devoted to in life.

But he wasn't really leaving for good.
He is remembered in his actions, his words,
and loved by people he hadn't seen in years.

With that kind of legacy,
you never really leave.
You remain present in a different forms–

in love, in people, in places.

I remember him fondly on quiet days,
and I've found that grief
is just love you couldn't place.

24/11. Dear Younger Me

I'm not where you dreamed to be,
but then again, you did dream big–
enormous, wonderful dreams
and I promise I'm running toward them.

But please, don't think about growing up right now.
Your life is beautiful,
the most wonderful gift,
and it all works out in the end.

Don't worry about me;
you'll be fine.
Just think about life as it is
and don't be scared to open up.
Granted, some people wouldn't
want to play with you,
but many are just waiting
for you to ask.
So take the chance:
it's great if it's a yes,
it's okay if it's a no–
the good news is,
you have seven billion tries
and only one life.

When you look in the mirror,
remember this:
you don't deserve to hate yourself like that.
You're beautiful–

in the way you think,
in the way you trust people.
The world has convinced
the prettiest of dolls
that they're ugly.
Don't go down that road.
Looks are the least of anyone's concerns.
You're part Mom and part Dad,
and you're going to be someone
always trying to be good
and that's all that matters.
So be good.
Be kind.
I'm doing the best with what I know,
and so did you.
And I know we love each other–
but we forget to love ourselves in the present.
So here's your reminder:
Take care.

Love,
Manjishtha

25/11. Sum Of All The People

I'm writing this poem
because I have my father's flair for writing.
I also have my mother's determination
and can only draw half as good as my sister.
My brother and I share a sense of humour
and I've got some kindness from dadu,
and the looks from dadi,
and the introversion from nana,
and the resilience from nani.
And I think that's how you're a living legacy–
an individual who is a story in their own right–
A tapestry of all those who came before
And a roadmap for those to come.

26/11. Red Thread of Destiny

A thread that ties us to people
we are destined to meet
intertwined and tangled
in our lives
and yet invisible.
but I feel like
the thread can guide you
but you're the one
who has to tug at it
pull the other end closer
and make sure you don't break it
because break needs knots
and a knotted thread
never makes for strong connections.

27/11. Beauty of Loneliness

I think there's a charm to
feeling absolutely,
utterly
lonely at times.

And hear me out–
I think that because
being lonely means
you're capable of love
beyond what you've given,
and you want a placeholder
for all of that warmth inside you.

You can't bottle the sun
and expect it to stop shining.
And I think you're the same.
Even in the darkest depths of despair,
there's a tiny ray of hope inside you
that you deserve to want to love someone.
And you do deserve intimacy,
affection,
kindness,
honesty,
and reciprocation.

And from that perspective,
you're not really alone, are you?
We can be lonely together
and wait
for the next person
who will hold our love.

28/11. Pomegranate Joy

Waiting for big milestones
might cause you to miss
the small joys of life
the little moments that make you
smile and appreciate where you are.
Stay
and feel that joy.
The big wins and grand celebrations can wait–
they are in the future
and you are in the present.
if you wait for joy
to come packaged
in the way you hoped
you might spend your life waiting.
So don't hesitate–
when happiness bursts into your life
like pomegranate seeds in your mouth.

29/11. Not sponsored by Nike

do it scared.
do it slow.
do it wrong.
do it worried.
do it flustered.
do it funny.
do it tired.
do it thoughtfully.
do it hasty.
do it hopeful.
do it right.
do it real.
do it excited.
do it exasperated.
do it amused.
do it ambitiously.
just don't stop to overthink–
it's either progress or experience
so take the leap
and just do it.

30/11. Things Fall Apart

If you are on the edge of your sanity,
and future appears closer to doom,
you've got to wait for the light to shine again
and with the knowledge of what despair looks like
you will be stronger to face the winds that await.
it's cliche I know, but here's a new way to look at it–
happiness in your life must be balanced out
by difficult moments that make you cherish
every little joy and achievement that follows.
loss of people makes you appreciate
all those who stick around for you.
loss of direction and clarity makes you value
every guiding sign and moments of eureka.
loss of things you love makes you grateful
for every new thing you get yourself.

so don't give up yet–
there is so much more on the horizon
waiting for you to come towards it
after you make it through this hard climb.
you are not going insane–
the world was never designed for sanity,
it keeps getting bigger and crazier and difficult to
navigate.
but remember that–

if things are falling apart now
they will fall into place soon.
trust in yourself,
all those with you,
before you
and the universe.
you will find your place–
and the victory is going to taste even sweeter
because you've seen devastating defeat.

01/12. Edge of 22

At the closing of the year,
and the beginning of December,
I am inching closer to completing
another year on the earth
and it's a crazy age to be–
when you're mentally stuck in teenage
and worried about your future adult life.
what helps me though is to not take anything
seriously–
that is the biggest wisdom
I can impart at the edge of 22.
you are but a speck of stardust on a little country
in a mini continent on a tiny planet
in a small solar system in the vast expanse of the
universe–
what are your biggest issues
in the grand scheme of things?
you are put on the earth to live
simply, to live.
there is no purpose to be found,
no impending doom,
no pot of gold at the end of rainbows
and for all we know, not anything after this.
which is also a lesson in gratitude–
you were born in this era,
with these people,
and culture that raised you,
merely by chance.

I know some of us have it worse than others,
and you cannot blindly ask people to be thankful for a
bad life–
to them, I am grateful you are alive and fighting,
I am grateful that you choose to hope for a better life
rather than give up–
I see you here and I appreciate you being here,
please hold the fort till things get better–
please live.